D1096523

Wandering Woman: Colorado

The Ultimate Road Trip: One Woman's
Journey Across the United States by Car

Julie Bettendorf

Contents

Introduction

"Not all who wander are lost."

Are you sure? I thought to myself, as I tried not to panic. I was a long way from anything familiar, but that was how it should be. I had driven thousands of miles on dusty, pothole-filled roads. It's often on the worst roads that you can discover something truly amazing.

My dusty CRV was parked beside me, containing one restless dog and a variety of snack bags, all empty by now. There were no buildings in sight, no cars or people or movement at all. Only the constant humming of the insects as they buzzed around my head.

I turned to my left – another straight road that trailed off into the distance. I glanced over to the right, then behind me – two more barely discernible roads stretched out into the abyss. I was in a four-way intersection with no signs, no sense of direction, and no sign of life for several miles. No cell service either, and that meant no GPS. Damn, I thought. I'm lost.

How did I get here? I couldn't help but feel like this little intersection was a cruel metaphor for life. I began to daydream, imagining each road might transport me back to a different time, a different role in my life, and a different me.

If I took the road from whence I came, it could lead me all the way back to Oregon, back to my cheating third husband, back to a life of loneliness and solitude. There is no greater loneliness than being married to someone who isn't actually present in your life.

If I took the road to my left, perhaps it could take me back to my career as a dental hygienist, a job I hated deep down in my soul. There is something so disengaging about cleaning teeth for a living. It's a disgusting, smelly way to get a paycheck. It pays well, which is great, but the best part is the huge gob of friends I enjoy to this day.

Or maybe the road to my right, yes – maybe that's the path, I imagined. Maybe it could take me back to my real treasure, my kids. Back to their smiling, innocent faces as toddlers, as they danced around the Christmas tree and their father and I were still married. Back when they still needed me for every little thing.

But, that was just it. I didn't feel needed anymore. My kids weren't toddlers anymore – they were both full-grown adults, and far too busy for me. My dental buddies were still working, but I wasn't. Dental hygiene had robbed me of the cartilage in my fingers, giving me severe, disabling arthritis. And, I wouldn't be returning to any more husbands either, because three marriages were quite enough for me.

All three of these paths, all three of these roles – the wife, the mother, and the dental hygienist – had seemingly been stripped from me within a year. I was lost and looking to find myself again.

The funny thing about this phrase, "not all who wander are lost" – is that, in my experience, wandering and being lost walk hand-in-hand with one another, and the expression can be flipped. In my experience, not all who are lost are wandering, and that is a real disservice to the beauty and clarity that the world has to offer.

When one becomes lost, wandering is the only option to guide oneself back to a path. After all, one could not come upon any dirt path at all without wandering.

I began wandering at an early age, both with my mind and with my feet. At eight years old, I was reading a book about archaeology and dreaming of one day seeing Egypt. I didn't follow a traditional path in high school either, going heavily into foreign languages, in hopes of one day using them.

At twenty-five years old, I divorced my first husband (the dental student who talked me into becoming a dental hygienist so I could work for him) and decided to give traveling a real shot. I took off for the Andes and Macchu Picchu, climbing up ancient Inca stone steps to reach the magnificent ruins.

Anyone who has been to Macchu Picchu will tell you there is something ethereal and deeply spiritual about the place. The ruins stretch out across the emerald green mountains, way up in the middle of the sky. Macchu Picchu gave me my first experience of feeling history. This trip inspired me to come back and complete a degree in archaeology, and I've been wandering ever since.

More travel followed including a backpack trip around Europe for three months, by myself, and trips to Britain, Italy, and Greece. I visited the burial places of Crusaders, mummies, and ancient kings. I happened upon the castle of my namesake in Bettendorf, Luxembourg, and wandered my way through European history.

My favorite excursion by far was finally seeing Egypt with my daughter in 2012. Just like my childhood dream envisioned, I rode a camel beneath the pyramids of Giza, with my head wrapped in some man's sweaty turban. It was perfect.

Traveling has always been my own personal antidote to pain. I went to Mexico after my first and second divorces, Canada after my third, and Italy after my dad died. Call it avoidance if you want, but I call it an accelerated form of healing in the purest sense of the word. I believe travel can heal your soul.

Wandering has always worked its wonders on me – made me feel renewed, rejoiceful, grateful, and purposeful. It's been my medicine.

So, as I stood in that intersection, I once again wondered how wandering had led me so astray this time. What the hell am I supposed to do now? It was then that I realized that one last path had not been considered yet – the path which stretched straight out in front of me. Which role does this represent? I pondered.

The answer smacked me in the face.

That last dirt road – the only path that could take me where I wanted to go, the only path that ever truly healed me or showed me the way – was the path of the traveler. The wife, the mother, and the hygienist roles – though valued in their time – were sitting in the bleachers now. It was time to welcome and enable my boldest, bravest, and perhaps most pivotal role yet:

The role of the Wandering Woman.

Welcome to Wandering Woman

This book is for you – the grieving empty nester mom, the begrudged housewife, the woman in need of a drastic change in her life. Really, this book is for anyone with a passion for traveling. If you feel lost with no sense of direction or purpose in life, that's a bonus – this book will be even more appealing to you. And lastly, if you're a man reading this book, congratulations for holding a book with the word woman in the title. You're contributing to gender equality, and that's pretty neat.

I decided to combine three of my dearest loves – travel, history, and archaeology – and put them into a book because I believe wandering has the power to change your life. I have been to many areas of the world and had too many outstanding experiences to list. However, by the time both my children had moved out in 2017, I had never

seen my own country – America. It was the perfect time to explore a new country (my own) and discover a new me at the same time.

So, I packed up my Honda CRV, along with some gear and my 14-year-old furry friend, Sadie. *Wandering Woman* is the chronicle of my journey across eleven states, discovering the joy of getting lost and finding myself along the way.

Why America ?

A merica, the beautiful? I sure think so, but I didn't realize just how beautiful our country is until I embarked on traveling across eleven western states in a year.

The United States offers everything for the discerning palate. From spectacular beaches, austere mountains, to rolling plains, our country has it all. It's difficult to comprehend just how large and impressive our scenery is, until you experience it first-hand, with the ultimate road trip.

I also realized just how much of our history is missing from U.S. history I was taught as a kid. The history of our country didn't begin with the pilgrims landing on Plymouth Rock in the 1600s. Our history is far more ancient, with rock art and archaeological sites dating back over 12,000 years.

We also owe a tremendous debt to early pioneers who tamed our land. The Mormons and other groups ventured into the great unknown with their families and their worldly possessions. Some of them pulled cumbersome handcarts across the country to settle in inhospitable, dangerous locations.

The goal of Wandering Woman is to bring history back to life and make it interesting again. I am presenting some famous sites, and many little-known ones. You will take the road-less-traveled with me, while we explore ghost towns, rock art sites, archaeological sites, and museums, to discover the colorful tapestry that is our country.

I present some history, including dates, but my goal is to present more of the real-life stories of history, including ghost stories, profiles in history, voices from the past, and moments in time, to give you, the reader, a deeper understanding of the context of history.

This is by no means an exhaustive list of places to visit. In fact, I encourage you to discover America for yourself, as I did, by making a trek across the land by car. You can explore as the early explorers did, just a little more comfortably, with a lot less hardship.

I hope you enjoy this book and take a little time out to discover our beautiful country, and maybe even discover yourself in the process.

Safe Travels,

Julie Bettendorf

Welcome to Colorado

The Centennial State

*C*olorado has a history of being visited by explorers, beginning with the Spanish in 1540. Zebulon Pike came in 1806, giving Pike's Peak its name. Last, but not least, is General William C. Fremont in 1843. Once you pay a visit to wonderful Colorado, you will understand why so many have come here.

5 things to love about Colorado:

Dazzling, snow-capped mountain peaks

Abundant wildlife including elk, bighorn sheep, moose, and deer

Colorful historic mining towns like Leadville and Cripple Creek

Stunning scenery and history of the Silver Thread Scenic Byway

World famous archaeological sites like Mesa Verde

Dreams of Colorado

"*If you want to see an awesome color, then go to Colorado. Its beauty is like no others."– **Unknown***

"*Each year, millions of skiers come to Colorado to experience its superb emergency medical facilities." – **Dave Barry***

"*Only a stone's throw from downtown Denver is an easy walk through time that leads past dinosaur tracks, bones, ripple marks, and other traces of Colorado's vanished life and ancient environments." – **Ralph Lee Hopkins***

Top Stuff to See in Colorado

Favorite Colorado Archaeological Sites:

- Mesa Verde
- Canyon of the Ancients National Monument

Favorite Colorado Ghost Towns:

- Animas Forks
- St. Elmo

Favorite Colorado Museums:

- Anasazi Heritage Center, Canyon of the Ancients National Monument
- Museum of the Mountain West, Montrose

Favorite Colorado Scenic Drives:

- Bachelor Historic Loop Tour, Creede

- Route of the Silver Kings, Leadville

W̶hen driving through Colorado, be on the lookout for:

Moose, bighorn sheep, elk, and deer, sometimes in the middle of the road

Early Colorado

Early Animas Forks, Colorado

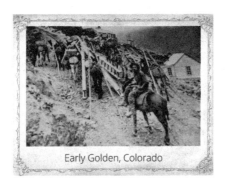
Early Golden, Colorado

Early Cripple Creek

Northern
Colorado

Georgetown, Colorado

Fort Vasquez

T he reconstructed ***Fort Vasquez*** is located right along the
highway, which makes it difficult to visualize what it must

have been like in the 1830s. The fort itself was very significant to the fur trade.

Fort Vasquez began its life in 1835 when fur traders, Louis Vasquez and William Sublette, applied for a trading permit from the superintendent of Indian Affairs, William Clark, of the Lewis and Clark expedition. The fort operated for 6 years trading goods with the Arapahoe and Cheyenne in exchange for buffalo robes and beaver pelts.

In the1850s, Fort Vasquez became a landmark to guide pioneers on the South Platte River Trail. In 1885, it became a stagecoach stop.

How to get to Fort Vasquez:

Fort Vasquez is located at 13412 US-85 in the town of Platteville.

Denver

D **enver** is home to the *9th Street Historic Park*, which has a section of historic brick buildings in superb condition.

The buildings include residences built from 1873 to 1905. Finch

The ***Colorado History Center*** is also in Denver. It's a fascinating museum with a large collection of artifacts from early Colorado. Among my favorites is license plate #2, made of leather and placed on the second automobile to come to Colorado.

Another one of my favorite items is the despondency vase from 1901. It's creator Artus Van Briggle, suffered from tuberculosis and commemorated his battle by creating the lovely vase. He died of the disease in 1904.

You can also enjoy a sparkling gold ingot from 1865. It belonged to Wilbur Fisk Stone, one of the many prospectors to work a placer claim in Colorado. The 5.6 ounce ingot was worth about $168 dollars when it was made.

Colorado History Center

Other artifacts include a Folsom Point, dated to between 11,700 and 12,900 years old, a whiskey flask from 1859, a buffalo hide overcoat from 1870, and Kit Carson's coat from 1853.

How to get to Denver historical sites:

The 9th Street Historic Park is located at 1068 W 9th Ave.

The Colorado History Center is located at 1200 N Broadway.

A moment in time:

The **Sand Creek Massacre** began on the morning of November 29, 1864, when members of the Colorado Militia attacked a group of Cheyenne and Arapahoe Indian families who were sleeping.

The militia was led by Colonel John Chivington, a former Methodist minister, who had sworn to kill all "women and children-killing savages."

The Indians, led by Chief Black Kettle, had been instructed to fly the American flag as a sign that they were friendly Indians.

Chivington ignored the flag, descending upon the Indian community and killing and mutilating approximately 150 Indians, many of whom were women and children. Chivington and his men would later march through Denver, carrying body parts of the slain Indians. [Donovan]

Chivington was court-martialed over the incident and allowed to resign his commission to avoid punishment. Black Kettle and his wife survived the Sand Creek Massacre, only to lose their lives four years later at the hands of George Armstrong Custer. [Crutchfield]

Voices from the past:

"To think of that dog Chivington up thar at Sand Creek! Whoever heerd of sich doings among Christians! Them pore Injuns had our flag flyin' over 'em. Well here come that durn Chivington and his cusses. They'd bin out huntin' hostile Injuns, and  *couldn't find none. So they just pitched into these friendlies and massa-creed them in cold blood. And ye call these civilized men Christians and the Injuns savages, du ye? Tain't natural for brave men to kill women and little children"* **Kit Carson, on Chivington's actions at Sand Creek.**

Golden

G olden may be most well-known for brewing Coors beer, but the city itself is pretty spectacular too. It's home to the *Golden History Park*, which is a beautiful outdoor park containing several historic buildings originally located on the historic Pearce Ranch near Golden.

The buildings include a schoolhouse, blacksmith shop, the Reynolds cabin, the Pearce cabin, a smokehouse, an outhouse, a chicken coop, and a barn. The buildings were disassembled and reassembled log-by-log on the park grounds.

The Reynolds Cabin, built in 1873, is the oldest building in the park.

Another wonderful structure is the Pearce Cabin, dating from around 1878. The Pearce family purchased the residence in 1919, and made it into their home.

Inside you will find a pump organ, bathtub, and other luxuries.

The schoolhouse was built in 1876 and contains one room. It stayed open until 1951.

Don't miss the adorable chickens wandering around the chicken coop.

How to get to Golden History Park:

Golden History Park is located at 1020 11th Street, in Golden.

Central City

*C**entral City*** is a quaint town, chock full of Victorian-style buildings and curving, graceful streets. Gold was discovered in nearby Clear Creek in 1859, and soon over 30,000 people moved into the area looking for gold. The area became known as "The Richest Square Mile on Earth." [Varney]

Central City got its name from being central to all of the mining camps in the area. The town also has the distinction of being the first town in the country to enjoy all electric street lighting by 1889.

Many interesting gold rush era buildings line the streets in Central City, including the *Teller House*, built in 1872. The ornate interior is unforgettable.

The *Opera House* is a majestic building built in 1878.

Don't miss the **Schoolhouse Museum** to get a fascinating look into the history of Central City through historical photographs.

How to get to Central City:

Central City is located about 35 miles west of Denver

Ghost story:

This is not quite a ghost story. I learned of this spooky true story from a helpful Visitor's Center employee. It seems an old Central City cemetery was located on a spot where a house was being built.

Coffins were excavated and the remains reinterred, but not before it was discovered that people had been buried while still alive. The inside of the coffins were covered with scratch marks. Back in the day, it was difficult to verify people were actually dead!

A word about mining terms and superstitions:

Some common terms thrown about in the world of mining include:

- **Prospecting**-looking for material to be mined, usually in the form of a gold or silver vein trapped within quartz. This is known as "blossom rock."

- **Placer mining**-to find superficial deposits of gold in streams and rivers

- **Lode mining**-to find deposits of precious metals enclosed in rock

Miners worked in extremely hazardous conditions, and the danger of their jobs may have led them to become highly superstitious. These are just a few of the superstitions miners believed in:

- Women were bad luck in the mines, especially if the woman was a redhead. It meant someone would die.

- Someone would also die if a black cat or a dog entered the mine.

- Whistling in a mine drove away good spirits and invited bad ones. Whistling was also believed to cause vibrations in the earth, prompting a cave-in.

- A cave-in was most likely to happen between midnight and 4 AM

- Miners would often quit a day early because they believed they would be injured or killed on their last shift Park City Museum

Profiles in history:

John Stetson, a hat maker, had tuberculosis. In 1860, he went out west to find a cure. He amazed his traveling companions by converting rabbit fur into felt fabric. From the fabric, he shaped himself a wide-brimmed, large hat to keep the sun out of his eyes and the rain off of his face.

When Stetson arrived in Central City, a horseman wanted his hat, so he bought the hat from Stetson. Stetson liked the look of the horseman as he rode off. Stetson returned to Philadelphia where he was from, but he couldn't get the look of the hat out of his mind.

He began to produce his "Boss of the Plains" hat. Soon, he had a new factory, producing thousands of hats. When Stetson died in 1906, he was making hundreds of thousands of hats each year. Stetson would be proud today to know that over 4 million Stetson hats are created and sold each year.

Georgetown

G *eorgetown* is a friendly, gorgeous town nestled in immense
mountains. It was founded in 1859, when two brothers,

George and David Griffith, found gold in nearby Clear Creek.
Georgetown was named after George, the older brother.

By 1880, Georgetown boasted a
population of 3000 people, and
had churches, hotels, schools,
and a large number of saloons.
The decline of Georgetown began in 1893 when silver prices
plummeted. Varney, Georgetown Visitor's Center

Today, Georgetown has some
wonderful historic buildings still
standing. The fabulous *Hotel de
Paris* is there, built in 1875.

You can also visit the *Old
Georgetown Station,* built
in 1877, *First Presbyterian
Church*, built in 1874, *Grace
Episcopal Church*, built in
1869, the *Old Jail*, built in the
1860s, and the *Hamill House*,
built in 1867.

When I visited Georgetown, the Hotel de Paris wasn't open for the season, but the kind man inside let me peek around a bit and take some photos.

The interior of the hotel is elegant and serene. It's the kind of place you could vacation in for the rest of your life.

You can also take a scenic drive through the *Guanella Pass Route*. The road winds past some spectacular views of Georgetown.

How to get to George-town:

Georgetown is located about 45 miles west of Denver, off of I-70.

Profiles in history:

Louis Dupuy was born in France under the name of Adolphe Francois Gerard. He immigrated to New York in 1868, when he was 22 years old. He joined the cavalry, bound for the Western states. After deserting the military in Cheyenne, he moved to Denver and changed his name to Louis Dupuy. He was a miner in Georgetown when he suffered an accident, retiring him from mining.

He then opened a bakery, creating elegant French pastries for the residents of Georgetown. The bakery turned into a full restaurant, and eventually the business became the Hotel de Paris, serving elegant French food on beautiful china.

The hotel was ahead of its time, having gaslights, and hot and cold running water in each room. Louis Dupuy died in 1900 and is buried in the cemetery north of Georgetown. He was 56 years old.

Silver Plume

***S**ilver Plume* is yet another lovely little ghost town high up in the mountains of Colorado. It was incorporated as a town in

1880, and soon had all the trappings of a town including saloons, shops, boarding houses, a school, a theatre, and churches.

The town got its name from the silver veins, which looked feathery within the stone. In 1884, a severe fire devastated the town, but the town was completely rebuilt by 1886. Silver Plume declined with the silver crash of 1893. [Varney]

Today the town still has the original stone jail with two cells, built in 1875. The jail closed in 1915.

Other buildings include a brick schoolhouse from 1894, *St. Patrick's Catholic Church* from 1874, and the *Brewery Spring House*.

Silver Plume also has a very picturesque cemetery, high up on a hill. A large pillar honors ten Italians, victims of an 1899 avalanche.

There are three small gravestones, each with a little lamb sitting on top. They are marking the tiny graves of Stella, Olwen, and Anna Laura Roberts, all younger than four years old. Life was hard for children back then.

How to get to Silver Plume:

Silver Plume is located only a few miles from Georgetown, off of I-70.

Ghost story:

Mad Jack lost his grip on sanity in 1859, causing his own death. His real name was John Strong, and he was a miner in Silver Plume. He and his mule both died in an accident. After he was buried, sounds of his pickaxe continued to be heard around the mine. His form has been seen, along with that of his mule.

Along with "Mad Jack" there is another ghost that haunts Silver Plume. His name was *Clifford Griffin*, an English bachelor, and he enjoyed playing the fiddle and drinking. Clifford led a tragic life. It seems his soon-to-be bride was strangled right before their wedding.

Clifford became a recluse, sitting alone in his cabin, but serenading the citizens of Silver Plume with his fiddle at night. As the years went by, Clifford became more crazed, and his music became more frenzied. Then, on the night of June 10, 1887, Clifford shot himself and fell into a crude grave he had carved out previously. His ghost can still be heard playing the fiddle in the hills above Silver Plume.  Waters

Central Colorado

St. Elmo, Colorado

Colorado Springs

*C*olorado Springs is home to the excellent *Pioneer Muse-um*, located in the old courthouse.

The museum houses an excellent collection of artifacts from Colorado Springs' early days, including a magnificent pair of pearl-handled opera glasses.

There is a fully furnished Victorian room for you to enjoy, along with old vehicles. Don't miss the toy room, with some fascinating tin toys.

To get to the second floor of the museum, you climb into an early Otis Birdcage Elevator from 1917. It can be an interesting trip. Sparks flew as I ascended upward.

How to get to the Pioneer Museum:

The Pioneer Museum is located at 215 S Tejon Street.

Ghost story:

Along Ute Pass, near Colorado Springs, there is a tunnel going through the pass known as the Widow Maker. Back in the day, a railroad engineer named **Michael Ryan** received a severe head injury. He was unable to work, so by 1900 he became a penniless hermit. He often walked by the side of the road carrying a railroad lantern.

By 1905, Ryan was living an isolated life in a shack, pelting intruders with rocks. He was declared insane by the court, and sentenced to live in an insane asylum in Pueblo, Colorado, from which he later escaped.

In 1923, deep inside the Widow Maker Tunnel, human remains were found, alongside a crushed railroad lantern. Officials determined that the bones were Michael Ryan's and he was buried where he lay, inside the tunnel. Today there are reports of flashes of light being seen at night, believed to be signals from long-dead railroad engineer Michael Ryan. Wommack

Cripple Creek

A n old story tells how ***Cripple Creek*** was named. Apparently, a cowboy chased a cow down into the creek. The end result was a broken arm for the cowboy, and a broken leg for both the horse and the cow. Someone was heard to remark "That is a cripple creek."

In the 1800s more gold was found in the Cripple Creek mining district than anywhere else in the world. Cripple Creek itself started to resemble a town in 1894. The area population grew from 15 people in 1890 to over 50,000 people 10 years later. Cripple creek was once Colorado's fourth largest city.

The Short Line Railroad, established in 1901 was 9 miles shorter than its competition, so it could make the trip from Cripple Creek to Colorado Springs in less time. In Monopoly, the "Short Line Railroad" is named after this Colorado railway.

Today, as you walk around Cripple Creek, you can visit the *Jail Museum*, which is housed in the *Teller County Jail*, used from 1901 until 1992.

Famous inmates included boxer Jack Dempsey, and Bob Lee, one of the Wild Bunch Gang.

There is a woman's section within the jail, containing all the niceties a woman in prison could want, including a footed bathtub and ornate porcelain sink.

Enjoy a tour of the *Mollie Kathleen Mine*, which includes a trip 1000 feet down into the mine, in a steel cage. Finch

How to get to Cripple Creek:

Cripple Creek is 60 miles west of Colorado Springs, off of Hwy 67.

A word about early medicine:

On the frontier, doctors weren't always readily available, so families often resorted to their own cures for ailments. For example:

For wart removal, rub the wart with bacon rind, green walnuts, or chicken feet.

For a toothache, scratch the gums with a nail until the gums bleed, then hammer the nail into a wooden beam.

For a child's teething pain, rub the child's gums with the warm brains of a freshly killed rabbit.

For a stomach ache, drink tea made from steeping dried chicken gizzard linings. [Enss]

Victor

T he town of *Victor* didn't suffer the same fate as the silver towns like Georgetown. Victor's claim to fame was gold, discovered in 1890.

Victor was named either for the Victor mine, or to honor homesteader Victor Adams. At the Portland Mine in Victor, one of the young mucker's names was William Dempsey, who became a boxer under his brother's name Jack Dempsey.

A miner's strike, deteriorating gold resources, and World War I all contributed to the decline of Victor. Today, you can visit the *Lowell Thomas Museum*, the *Isis Theatre, Victor Hotel*, and several other gold rush era buildings. Varney

When you tour Victor, be sure and visit the picturesque *Sunnyside Cemetery*. Outside the cemetery fence lies *Potter's Field*, where small white crosses mark the burials of Victor's unknown poor.

How to get to Victor:

Victor is located 6 miles southeast of Cripple Creek, off of Hwy 67.

Ghost story:

Thomas Dunn had a mortuary business on the first floor of the Dunn Building in Victor. It seems Dunn and an assistant were preparing a miner's body for burial. The miner was the victim of a cave-in and his body was horribly mangled.

During preparations, the man began twitching, and then screaming. The man, thought to be dead, was reaching to touch his eye, that was no longer there. Dunn gave the poor man a dose of morphine and continued his preparations, assuming that the man would eventually die, which he did.

Today there are reports of exploding light bulbs, slamming doors, and cold spots. Is it the poor unfortunate miner, or Thomas Dunn haunting the place? No one knows, but the words "Undertaker" still remain painted on the side of the building to remind us of Thomas Dunn and the poor miner. [Wommack]

South Park City

S outh Park City began its life in 1861 as a mining town known
as Fair Play. The name was changed to South Park City in

1869, but that name only lasted five years, when the name again became Fair Play.

It was shortened to just one word in 1924. Placer gold deposits were exhausted in the late1880s.
Varney

Today, as you walk around South Park City, you can enjoy 34 buildings, some of which are original to the site, and others which have been moved from various locations in the area. The buildings range in date from 1874 to 1929.

One of my favorites is the imposing *Fairplay School*, built in 1881.

How to get to South Park City:

South Park City is located at 100 4th Street, in the town of Fairplay.

A word about mail order brides:

The aftermath of the Civil War and the movement West for the Gold Rush led to a scarcity of men in the Eastern United States. The hardships of living in mining camps and prospecting was not a great environment for women either, so there were too many men and too few women in the West. Published numbers state the ratio was sometimes as great as 200 men to 1 woman. Business-minded people began what was known as the "mail-order bride" industry.

A well-read newspaper known as the Matrimonial News listed advertisements for women seeking to marry men, and for men seeking to marry women. Here are two of the more striking examples of ads from January 1887:

"A good looking young lady of 19, 5 feet 3 inches high, black hair and eyes, would like to find someone to love."

"I want to know some pretty girl of 17 to 20 years. I am 29, 5 feet 9 inches tall, a blonde: I can laugh for fifteen minutes and I want some pretty girl to laugh with me."

And from the New Plan Company Catalog, September 1917:

"Winsome Miss of 18 years, considered attractive looking, have many friends, very pleasant and lively, blue eyes, dark hair, fair complexion, good education, good cook and house-keeper, weight 130, height 5 feet; would make the right man a good wife; have a profit of $10,000; will answer all letters containing stamps."

"Would like to correspond with a farmer about 30 to 35 years old. Am an American widow of 33; height 5 feet, 2 inches; weight 200; brown eyes; brown hair; common school edu-cation. Personal property worth $1500. Object matrimony. No flirts need write." [Enss]

Leadville

*L**eadville*** began its life in 1877, when silver was discovered. The silver was contained in lead carbonate ore material, giving the town of "Leadville" its name. The town sits at an altitude of over 10,000 feet.

Leadville contains many historic buildings, including the ***Tabor Opera House***, built by Horace Tabor, a new silver millionaire. The Opera House opened its doors in November 1879. ^{Varney,}
Herald Democrat

As you walk around town, you can also visit the ***Old Presbyterian Church***, built in 1889, the ***Tabor Grand Hotel***, built in 1884, and the ***Western Hardware Building***, built in 1881.

Be sure and step inside the hardware building to talk a walk down memory lane.

These and other outstanding historic buildings are in excellent condition and can be seen on Harrison street through the historic downtown area.

While in Leadville, you should also visit the *National Mining Hall of Fame and Museum* in a Victorian school building built in 1899.

The *Gold Rush Room* in the museum was set up in part by the Gates Foundation. You can check out some gold nuggets, early mining history, and historical photos including one of the Ice Palace from the 1895 Winter Carnival.

Some of my favorite artifacts from the mining museum are an old miner's hat from the 1800's, and cages for the canaries the miners took down into the mines with them.

You can also visit the historic *Evergreen Cemetery*, a peaceful repository for early Leadville residents.

When in Leadville, you should also take the time to drive the *Route of the Silver Kings*, a scenic drive up into the mountains, past many old mining sites and Leadville history. Watch out for wildlife on the road.

While touring Leadville, be sure and look out for the colorful fences, creatively made out of old skis.

How to get to Leadville:

Leadville is located about 100 miles from Denver, off of I-70 and Hwy 91.

Profiles in history:

Horace Tabor and his wife *Augusta* opened several businesses around Leadville, and he grubstaked prospectors in their search for riches. Two prospectors found a huge silver deposit, and Tabor's share made him a rich man.

He divorced his wife Augusta, to marry an attractive, sought-after woman named *Elizabeth Doe*, nicknamed Baby Doe. The scandal rocked the town of Leadville. Augusta was given a paltry sum of $300,000 dollars from Tabor's net worth of over 9 million dollars.

Tabor and Baby Doe overspent on luxuries. Combined with the silver crash, they ended up penniless. Horace died in 1899, advising Baby Doe to keep the Matchless Mine in Leadville, thinking it was going to eventually make her rich.

Baby Doe died alone in a cabin next to the Matchless Mine; her lifeless body was found in March 1935. Augusta, the ex-wife, invested the $300,000 wisely. She died in 1895, at the age of 62, leaving an estate worth 1.5 million. Crutchfield

Voices from the past:

"*Scarcely had any snow sifted in, although the cabin had been covered by the slide to a depth of fifty feet. The stillness of death prevailed the single room, although three human forms sat there as in life, and outlines of another silhouetted against the strange light in the bunk yonder, wrapped in a wakeless sleep. This was Jack Carroll.*

Sitting opposite each other at a table, with cards before them and in their hands, were Summers and Temple... On the opposite side of the room, at a little table, sat your son Albert, as life-like as when I had last seen him. He had been engaged in writing a letter to you, and when the awful shock came, his hand was still holding the pen..."

Letter from Joshua Watson, Leadville postmaster dated March 9, 1882 to Mrs. William Morrison, telling her of the death of her son, Albert, buried in a snowslide along with three companions. Victims of the avalanche are buried in Leadville's Evergreen Cemetery, with the grave marked by a large memorial statue. *Coquoz*

A moment in time:

The magnificent *Ice Palace* was built for the Leadville Winter Carnival of 1895. It was begun in November of 1895, and opened on New Year's Day 1896. The Ice Palace cost over $140,000 to build and required over 5,000 tons of ice and 250 laborers.

The structure was huge, measuring 450 feet long and 320 feet wide, covering 5 acres. Ice blocks were cut from the surrounding lakes and hauled to the site, where they were put together to form solid walls. The ice palace contained turrets, an indoor skating rink, a restaurant, and a ballroom. It began to melt in March of 1896, and was completely gone by June of the same year. Leadville Mining Museum

St. Elmo

St. Elmo is the real deal when it comes to ghost towns. I visited when the snow was still thick on the ground, almost covering the windows of many of the buildings. The wooden sidewalks creaked under my feet as I walked along, giving the place a spooky feeling.

St. Elmo began its life in 1879, named after a popular novel of the period. Gold and silver were found in the area of Chalk Creek nearby, causing the population to soar.

The mines eventually declined and were closed, and St. Elmo became the ghost town it is today.
Varney

You can visit over 40 historical structures including a *Miner's Exchange* and the *Home Comfort Hotel*, built in 1885.

A word of warning: the road to St. Elmo is an old railroad grade. You will think you are driving up into the middle of nowhere, but St. Elmo is up the road, so keep going. This ghost town is well worth the trip.

How to get to St. Elmo:

St. Elmo is located 19 miles from the town of Nathrop, off of County Road 162.

Ghost story:

There is a legend about ***Tommyknockers*** that are said to haunt many mining camps. Tommyknockers got their name from Cornish miners who believed that little men lived underground and caused the knocking with their tiny hammers.

Some early miners believed Tommyknockers were good spirits who were warning of an impending mine collapse. Others believed that the person who heard the knocking would die. Still others believed that Tommyknockers were the spirits of miners who had died during a cave-in. Some miners even left offerings of food and drink to appease the Tommyknockers.

Southwestern
Colorado

Animas Forks, Colorado

Montrose

***M**ontrose* is home to the famous *"Hangin' Tree"* where, on August 9, 1878, "George Bikford was strung up for robbery and horse stealin". Bikford was once part of the Dalton gang. The next morning a burial party was sent out, but they couldn't find the body. ^{Town of Montrose}

Montrose also has the fabulous ***Museum of the Mountain West***. It's a wonderful indoor/outdoor museum with an amazing array of historical buildings.

My favorites are buildings you could order from the Montgomery Ward catalogue, back in the day, and then put them together yourself.

The museum houses a half-million artifacts from the years 1880 to 1930, including my favorite, a Wrigley's gum dispenser.

This museum is a great way to spend an afternoon.

How to get to Montrose:

Montrose is located in Western Colorado, off of Hwy 50.

Ouray

***O** uray* is a quaint and beautiful historic town, established in 1875, and nestled high in the mountains.

Large silver deposits were discovered south of Ouray in 1881.

There are some excellent eater-
ies and gift shops to peruse, along
with historic buildings.

The *Ouray County Historical Museum* is housed in the
old mining hospital, first opened
in 1887. The museum has an
excellent collection of artifacts
arranged on three levels.

There is a toy room, housing children's toys, a Native American room, housing a nice collection of Ute artifacts, a railroad room, veteran's room, and old law office.

My favorite rooms are the dental office, containing the first dental chair used in Ouray, and the operating suite, containing a frightening old x-ray machine, and terrifying surgical tools from the 1890s.

Outside of the museum, you can also enjoy pioneer structures, including the *McIntyre Cabin*, built in 1878.

It's furnished with period items from 1878-1896. The McIntyre family were early settlers in Ouray county. Ouray County Historical Society

How to get to Ouray:

Ouray is located 40 miles north of the city of Montrose.

Fun fact:

The popsicle was invented in Ouray in the 1920s.

Lake City

I f heaven was a town, it would surely be *Lake City.* It's tree-lined streets, peppered with exquisitely restored historic houses, is a joy to see.

The town began when Enos Hotchkiss, along with his companions, discovered large mineral deposits in 1874. This discovery would later become known as the Golden Fleece Mine.

By 1875 Lake City became the county seat. The Denver & Rio Grande Railroad came to town in the 1880s, causing the town to boom. Eventually Lake City had five saloons, three restaurants, three breweries, five stores, two bakeries, two meat markets, drugstores, a library, and a newspaper. The town declined from the silver crash of 1893. Varney

Many of the original owners of the historic houses of Lake City have interesting histories like these:

An owner of one house died of a lung abscess in 1912 after his horse fell on him. He was on his way to the Black Crook Mine.

An owner supplemented her income by selling whiskey during prohibition days.

An owner died during the Spanish Flu epidemic in 1920.

An owner was suspected of poisoning another man with cyanide.

One house was used to quarantine people during the swine flu epidemic of 1918-1920.

There are so many historic buildings in Lake City, it's easier to just list them:

- The *Hinsdale County Museum*
- The 1877 *Stone Bank Block*
- The 1883 *Opera House*
- The 1880 *Hough Block*
- The 1877 *Hinsdale County Courthouse*
- The 1877 *John Hough House*

- The 1877 *Turner House*

- The 1892 *Steinbeck-Nettleton House*

- The 1892 *Youman's House*

- The 1876 *Episcopal Chapel*

- The 1876 *Presbyterian Church*

- The 1891 *Baptist Church*

- The 1878 *St. Rose of Lima Catholic Church*[Houston]

Don't miss the *Lake City Cemetery*, with its ornate metal scrollwork fencing.

Another fascinating stop is the *Alferd Packer Massacre Site*. It was here in 1874 that Alferd Packer is said to have murdered five men he was guiding from Lake City to Gunnison.

The site is marked by five small white crosses and a plaque with the names of the five unfortunate men. Lake City/Hinsdale County Mar‗keting Committee

How to get to Lake City:

Lake City is located in south-western Colorado, 55 miles south of the city of Gunnison, on Hwy 149.

Profiles in history:

Alferd Packer was a guide whose specialty was leading people through the San Juan Mountains. In November 1873, a group of Utah prospectors hired him. Two months later, Packer emerged from the mountains, alone. He claimed he got separated from the prospectors and had nearly starved.

A group of men set out in search of the missing men and found them. All had been either hacked to death with an axe or shot. The men's remains had been butchered. Suspicion of murder and cannibalism fell on Packer, who had since fled out of town. Packer was arrested in 1883 and returned to Lake City for trial. He was sentenced to death. For-

tunately for Packer, his sentence was reduced to prison, and he was paroled after a few years. He died near Denver in 1907.

Silverton

S *ilverton* has two stories of how the town got its name. It's either a shortened version of Silvertown, or it was named by a miner shouting there was "silver by the ton."

The town was first named Baker's Park, named after Captain Charles Baker, who came into the area in 1860.

The Denver & Rio Grande railroad came into Silverton in 1882, which helped the population grow and made shipping of precious metals much cheaper.

Silverton's main production started out as silver, but gold, lead, and copper soon followed.
Varney

As you walk around Silverton, you can see several historic buildings, including the 1902 *County Jail*, which is now a museum, the 1906 *San Juan County Courthouse*, and the *Wyman Hotel*, built in 1902.

You can also see the *Town Hall*, built in 1908, and the *Original Jail* from 1883.

You can pick up a handy walking tour map at most of the Silverton shops.

Silverton is also home to the excellent ***San Juan County Historical Museum***, which houses a wonderful collection of early Silverton artifacts including furnishings, mining items, and historical photographs.

There are also furnished historic cabins on the grounds of the museum.

The Durango & Silverton Narrow Gauge Railroad also runs out of Silverton, so the town can get quite busy and full of tourists, especially during the summer months.

How to get to Silverton:

Silverton is located one hour south of the city of Montrose.

Animas Forks

A nimas Forks is in spectacular surroundings, as are most of the ghost towns in Colorado.

The town was founded in 1873, and got its name because three rivers met at a camp known as Three Forks, also known as Forks of the Animas. The town name was shortened to Animas Forks.

The town sits at an elevation of over 11,000 feet, so winters were treacherous. The town began to decline in 1891. Animas Forks has about 10 buildings which still have roofs.

In Animas Forks, you can see one of the most photographed ghost town buildings in Colorado, the *William Duncan Home*, built in 1879, by William Duncan, a miner from Pennsylvania.

The house has some unusual features, including tall bay windows, to view the spectacular mountains.

The Duncans left Animas Forks in 1884, lasting only five years in the remote town. They left behind a spectacular homestead.

Another wonderful building is the *Charles and Alma Gustavson House*, built in 1906. Charles bought the land for $1.00 and the house was built. The Gustavson House has unusual features too, including an "indoor toilet" which was actually an outhouse with a closed half door, and a root cellar.

The Gustavsons sold the house in 1910 for $110.00.

My favorite building is the *Jail*, built in 1882.

It boasts walls that are six inches thick and bars on the windows and doors. [Varney]

How to get to Animas Forks:

Animas Forks is located 12 miles from Silverton, off of County Road 2.

A word about preservation:

Many ghost towns are not restored. Instead, they undergo a process known as "arrested decay." The buildings are only repaired and stabilized to prevent them from collapsing, but they are not restored.

Efforts are made to stabilize rock foundations and repair leaking roofs to prevent further damage, but the buildings are left in their original condition at the time of purchase.

Creede

Creede began its life in 1890 late into the silver boom. In fact, the silver crash would happen only three years later. The town was named after Nicholas Creede, who discovered silver in 1889. He founded what would be called the Holy Moses claim.

By 1893, Creede's population had risen to about 10,000 people. Var-ney

As you walk around Creede, you can see the 1891 ***Railroad Depot***, which is now a museum, and the ***Bachelor Cabin***. This cabin was moved from the now abandoned town of Bachelor to Creede, and reassembled piece-by-piece.

One of my favorite Creede sights is a ***Jail Cell*** from Creede's first jail.

The real star of Creede is the **_Bachelor Historic Tour_** scenic drive. You can pick up a booklet at the Creede Visitor's Center on Main Street. This is a must-do in my opinion, whether you are in Creede, or in Colorado.

The drive is spectacularly beautiful, but does require a high-clearance vehicle. Four wheel drive is best. My CRV is all-wheel drive and it made the trip just fine.

The nice lady in the Visitor's Center recommended I drive the tour backwards, so I would be going down the steep, twisting area known as Black Pitch instead of climbing it. She gave me some excellent advice.

One of the first mining claims was in 1883, at what would become the *Commodore Mine*. It's an imposing site, with over 200 miles of tunnels. It's #2 on the tour route.

#3 on the tour is the steep stretch of road known as *Black Pitch*. It became a graveyard for mules, horses, and wagons which plunged to their deaths over this area. The dead animals and wagons were burned to get them out of the way for later travelers.

#4 on the tour is the *Weaver Townsite*, which once held several hundred inhabitants.

The *Last Chance Mine*, #11.5 on the tour, is my personal favorite. It was discovered in 1891, by a man named Renniger who went looking for his lost burros. He found the burros, but couldn't get the burros to move, so the man sat down and began to dig with his pick.

He found rich mineral deposits and asked Nicholas Creede to come see. Creede was so impressed he established his claim next to Renniger's. Renniger named his mine Last Chance, in honor of his burros.

The owners of the mine offer lodging in fantastic cabins perched on the hillside with out-of-this-world views.

There is also a great seating area to relax and enjoy the spectacular surroundings. The Last Chance Mine also offers underground tours which are highly informative and fun.

I spent the night at the Last Chance Mine in a cozy cabin clinging to the hillside.

The bed was comfy, and the cabin was immaculate. A woodstove kept me warm on the chilly mountaintop.

#12 the ***Bachelor Townsite***, is now just a grassy meadow, but it once was a town of about 1000 people.

Bachelor City, at an elevation of 10,500 feet, was known as the "town in the clouds."

#15 on the tour is the ***Creede Cemetery***, a picturesque little spot.

#16 on the tour is ***Bob Ford's Gravesite***. Bob Ford's remains were unearthed and shipped back to Missouri by his widow, in 1892. Willow Creek Reclamation Committee

How to get to Creede:

Creede is located about 265 southwest of Denver off Hwy 285.

A moment in time:

The year was 1882, when ***Bob Ford*** shot Jesse James in the back in Missouri, killing him. He knew the James gang would come after him, so he fled and ended up in Creede, Colorado, opening up a gambling and dance hall.

One evening, Ford was standing at his bar, trying to raise money for a funeral for one of his dancing girls who had killed herself with an overdose of morphine. A man named O'Kelley, who was the marshal of nearby Bachelor City came in. O'Kelley had grown up in Missouri and knew Jesse and the James Gang.

He recognized Ford, and shot him in the head and neck, killing Ford instantly. O'Kelley received a life sentence, but was later pardoned in 1902, after serving 10 years of his sentence. O'Kelley died two years later, as a result of a fight with an Oklahoma City police officer. [Enss]

Mesa Verde

***M*esa Verde** is one of the world's best known archaeological areas and includes over 4500 archaeological sites, 600 of which are cliff dwellings.

It was discovered when Richard Wetherill, a local rancher, saw the cliff palace on December 18,1888.

Native people first came into the area around 550 CE, living in pit houses for 700 years before abandoning their dwellings in the 1200s.

Ancestral Puebloan people began building the cliff dwellings between the late 1190's to late 1270's.

They lived in the dwellings for less than 100 years, abandoning them by 1300 CE.

The *Spruce Tree House* is the best preserved cliff dwelling, built between 1211 and 1278. It has 130 rooms, 8 kivas, and housed 60 to 80 people.

The structure was named by explorers in 1888, for the large spruce trees in the canyon below.

The Spruce Tree House was abandoned between 1280 and 1300, possibly due to a large scale drought from 1276 to 1299, which was revealed by tree rings. Noble, National Park Service

The spectacular *Cliff Palace* is the largest cliff dwelling in North America. Ancestral Puebloans moved into the houses in 1200 AD.

The Cliff Palace has 150 rooms, 75 open spaces, and 21 kivas. Much of it was built in 20 years between 1260-1280 CE. Tree ring dating shows a span from 1209-1280, with some dates as early as 1190-91CE.

100 to 120 people called the Cliff Palace home. Ancients climbed down from the mesa into the structures with hand and toe holds carved into the cliff. Mesa Verde Museum Association

Mesa Verde has an excellent **Visitor Center** and **Museum**. The many artifacts include 1500 year-old ears of corn, a winter boot made of turkey feathers, and stunning black-on-white pottery.

How to get to Mesa Verde:

Mesa Verde is in Southwestern Colorado, off of Hwy 160, about 35 miles west of Durango.

Voices from the past:

*"strange and in the mysteri-
ous twilight of the cavern, and
defying in their sheltered site
the ravages of time, it resem-
bles at a distance an enchanted
castle"* **Gustav Nordenskiold,
Swedish scientist and early
visitor to Mesa Verde, 1891.**

A word about what happened:

What happened to these ancient cultures which caused them to abandon their monumental buildings:?

• The Mimbres culture disappeared around 1130 AD.

• Chaco Canyon and Ancestral Puebloan disappeared middle to late 1100's.

• Mesa Verde and Kayenta cultures disappeared around 1300 AD.

• Mogollon culture disappeared around 1400 AD.

• Hohokam disappeared late into the 1400's.

It was probably a combination of factors that caused the residents to abandon their homes. One of the main causes was a major mul-ti-year drought beginning around 1130 AD. Cultures were impact-ed differently by this, depending on whether they lived in an area with more or less rainfall. Those that lived at higher elevations with more rainfall tended to cope with the drought better.

Cultures with larger populations like Chaco Canyon, exhausted their food supply more quickly, resulting in conflict over food, land, and other resources. There is some evidence of cannibalism, because human muscle protein has been found in the dried fecal material of ancient humans. Major conflict was inevitable, and it is widely believed that ancient survivors were absorbed into other cultures like the Zuni. Diamond

Canyon of the Ancients

*C*anyon of the Ancients National Monument contains the superb *Anasazi Heritage Center* which contains many beautiful examples of Mesa Verdean style black on white pottery.

Other interesting artifacts are numerous pendants of various materials, and a turkey-feather blanket.

One of my favorite artifacts is a set of painted mural fragments.

A path outside the Heritage Center takes you past the *Dominguez and Escalante Pueblos*, both built in the 1100s. They are named after the two Franciscan priests who camped near the area while searching for a route from Sante Fe, New Mexico, to the California missions.

The ***Lowry Pueblo*** is another site within the monument. It contains a spectacular kiva, with stone blocks placed to represent what some believe are figures of winter and summer people.

You can see slight traces of light blue, black, and white paint on the walls.

Another interesting feature of Lowry Pueblo are the lines of dark stone, creating a linear design in the walls.

Lowry Pueblo imitates the Chacoan style of architecture, with blocked-in kivas, yet Chaco is 125 miles away, demonstrating how far Chacoan culture had spread.

Many of the buildings have several evenly spaced openings in the walls, which once held wooden beams to support a second floor.

There were five building periods at Lowry, with the main building occurring between 1085 and 1090 CE. Lowry Pueblo was named for an early homesteader named George Lowry.

How to get to Canyon of the Ancients:

Canyon of the Ancients National Monument is located about 10 miles from the city of Cortez.

A word about kivas:

The word "kiva" means cellar or underground house, and it was a special place of ceremony. Kivas were used primarily by men, but women and children could enter them for certain ceremonies and at certain times.

When an area was abandoned, kivas were often ritually closed by being filled in and sealed, and the roofs were burned.

Favorite Places to Stay

Last Chance Mine

L*ast Chance Mine Cabins*–located on the Bachelor Loop Historic Tour, beginning in Creede, Colorado. There are a few outstanding cabins which are converted shipping containers.

The interiors are cozy, clean, and comfortable, with woodstoves to keep you warm. Staying at the Last Chance MIne and taking the tour are an experience not to missed, and the views are world-class. For more information, call *(719) 238-7959*, or email *jack@lastchancemine.com.*

View from the Argo Inn terrace

Argo Inn and Suites–located in Idaho Springs, Colorado. It's a great location to tour surrounding towns like Georgetown, Silver Plume, and others. The rooms are clean, comfortable, and have terraces overlooking the river. Bighorn sheep come down to drink and you can view them from the terrace. For more information, check out the website at *argoinnandsuites.com*.

Animas Forks, Colorado

Dispersed and paid camping–located in most areas of Colorado outside the large cities. You can check out dispersed camping locations on the Uncover Colorado website at ***www.uncovercolorado.com***. Colorado is also home to a wealth of stunning state parks. You can check them out at ***cpw.state.co.us***.

Random Thoughts

What History Means to Me

F irst, let me start by sharing with you my opinion of what history isn't. History is not a collection of random dates, names, and places for you to memorize. History is not a dry and uninteresting class you have to pass to graduate.

I believe history is a tangible thing. You can actually *feel* history in the places you go, and the sights you see. I remember walking up to the Acropolis in Athens. I looked down at the well-worn marble steps and wondered about how many ancient philosophers had climbed these very steps, thousands of years ago.

You don't have to go far away to experience the *feeling* of history. If you are lucky enough to live in an old house, you may experience history in your own surroundings. You might say to yourself, *"If only these walls could talk."*

During my travels across the United States, I *felt* history in many, many places. If you travel across the country like I did, you will *feel* the wonderful history of our beautiful country for yourself, and you will never be the same. You will discover what it means to be an American.

Why I did it and why you can too:

I decided to travel across the country by car because I wanted to rediscover America. When I first set out to explore the history of our country, I wanted to find out why America is the greatest country on earth, and what it means to be an American.

The politics of these United States was frightening at the time. Our country was polarized, almost beyond repair. Whether it was Democrats or Republicans, Conservatives, or Liberals, everyone was fighting.

I wanted to rediscover the joy of being an American. I wanted to rediscover our rich history, our unique and wonderful people, our tapestry of multicultural heritage, and our rich natural resources. I thought a road trip by car across eleven western states was a good place to start.

I have a degree in Archaeology, and a passion for all things archaeological. I love history, with a side love of paleontology. It is these three passions that I set my trip agenda around. I set out to discover the archaeological sites, history, and paleontological world of our country.

As I travel and write my books, I get asked all the time, especially by women, "What is it like to travel by yourself? Aren't you scared?" The truth is, I believe everyone should do what I did. It's a wonderful way to discover our country, and to rediscover yourself. The truth is, I'm scared not to travel. Traveling allows you to get to know yourself, in ways not possible when sitting on the couch watching TV.

We tend to spend a lot of our lives tuning out the world and our place within it. When you travel, you are quite literally forced to deal with your own thoughts, emotions, and feelings. You can discover yourself while traveling. You can come to understand what makes you who you are, and how you can perhaps become a better person. Above all, traveling gives you mental clarity to figure out how to live with intent. It's a way to guide your life, not just wait for things to happen.

Travel Tips & Stuff

What You Need to Know

How to get started:

P lanning your trip should be one of the most exciting things about it. You want to be spontaneous, but it is also very wise to plan your route, so you can take full advantage of all the time and miles you will invest.

First, decide your passions. If you love airplanes, trains, or old vehicles, plan your trip around that. If you love gardens or architecture, seek that out as the focus of your trip.

Next, read and research areas of the country that will let you enjoy what you are interested in.

Make a list by state and city or town, of what you want to see.

Take your handy road atlas and locate the areas on the pages.

Make a tentative route plan, so you have an idea of where you are going.

Travel tip: Avoid trying to plan your trip down to a schedule of days, hours, or minutes. On a road trip, it will be virtually impossible to know where you will be on any given day. If you adhere to a schedule, you are more likely to stress out, and less likely to actually enjoy yourself, which is the whole point.

What you need:

You need to bring along a sense of adventure and a curious mind. You need to ditch the idea of always being on a schedule, and live a little more spontaneously to thoroughly enjoy yourself. Things will happen as you travel, both good things and bad things, and you need to prepare your mind and your soul for day-to-day changes.

So much of our lives are planned out. Between growing up, going to school, finding a career, marriage, kids, or whatever, people have lost much of the ability to be spontaneous. But you must take spontaneity on the trip with you, because you may make detours along the way to see something really spectacular.

So, for the practical stuff you need:

A great vehicle-I have a Honda CRV which is fabulous. It's old, a 2004, fully paid for, and will go anywhere. I see humongous RVs on the road, towing a car behind, and all I can think of is, they can't go just anywhere. They are too big. Bad gas mileage, cumbersome to drive, slow, and not agile like my CRV. So, I encourage you, if you want to go car camping and be able to go on remote dirt roads, get an agile vehicle, and Hondas are great.

Travel tip: Don't be afraid to do some modifications to your vehicle. I took one of my back seats out. (after watching a YouTube video) I threw in a twin mattress, a bit of drapery, and some netting. I also put some of those little portable light switches on the inside. I jettisoned anything I hadn't used up to that point. Don't be afraid to get rid of unnecessary stuff.

An awesome camera that you know inside and out. I use a Nikon and it takes wonderful pictures. Don't skimp on a camera, and don't think a cellphone camera is all you need, because you want the best for your beautiful photos.

A hot plate warmer-this little item was indispensable. You need a converter for it so you can plug it in to the cigarette lighter. Place your food inside it, carton and all, and then plug it in. 30 minutes for thawed food, about an hour and a half for frozen food. Boom! You have a hot meal by the time you stop for the night!

Window shades-the best ones are magnetic so you just place them against your windows and they cling to them, obscuring the view inside your car.

Portable cooler with wheels-another indispensable item that works great and is easy to move around. I use those nifty blue frozen blocks in mine.

Portable air compressor-this little gem plugs into your cigarette lighter and will inflate your tires if you have a flat. Fortunately, I haven't had to use this yet.

Portable battery charger and power bank-mine comes with battery cables and the power bank, yet once inside the case, it is small enough to put in your glove compartment. This little item, unfortunately, I have had to use, and it saved me.

Portable generator-mine came with a small solar panel, so it can be charged with solar or electricity. It has a decent battery life and also doubles as a light for night-time.

All season clothing-you never know what different states will bring for weather, so take hot weather and cold weather clothes, and a fair amount of shoes appropriate for hiking, or walking, sandals, and slippers, which are nice at night. Also take along a pair of cheap rubber flip-flops to wear in the public showers you might go into.

Your own pillows-I like my own pillows, so I don't wake up with neck cramps, especially after sleeping in the car.

Sleeping bag and cozy blankets-you want to stay warm and layering is everything.

Warm hat, warm socks, and fuzzy jammies to keep you warm for cold nights sleeping in the car.

A great road atlas, and great guidebooks-get one that's easy to read, with great pictures. For a road atlas, just get one that is easy to read.

A word about photography:

Along with a great camera, you need to have a great eye. This is easier than it sounds once you have worked with your camera and are comfortable taking pictures with it. I am not a professional photographer, but I like my pictures and other people do too.

These are my tips for taking great pictures:

- Experiment with taking both horizontal and vertical shots.

- Don't always put the subject of the photo in the middle of the photograph.

- This one is important: pay attention to the foreground, and if possible, have something, a plant or whatever, in the foreground to help give the photo dimension and depth.

- This one is important too: turn around often to see the view you just came from. I do this quite often and some of my best pictures have resulted from when I turned around and took the shot.

You can also take a mental photo. Place an image in your mind that you can call upon later. Use all of your senses to see, hear, smell, and maybe even to taste, what is around you. You have the means to fully experience your surroundings, and that is very important to a traveler. When you take a mental photo, be sure to jot down quick little details about what you saw, heard, smelled, or tasted, so you can jog your memory later.

And last, but not least...don't be posing in front of everything, everywhere, to show that you actually went somewhere. Most people want to see themselves in your photo and be mentally transported there, but they can't if you are there already.

To camp or not to camp:

Car camping is great. I prefer it to sleeping on the cold, hard ground in a tent. I can lock the doors, put my window shades up and be cozy for the night.

That being said, for me there were some do's and don'ts about camp sites. Some people camp in a Walmart parking lot and feel safe. I do not. I believe that if you are in a busy area, you're more likely to be confronted by a nut job who may bother you. Nothing against Walmart.

Same goes for casino parking lots. Many people believe that if they are in a public place, there is less chance of someone bothering them. I don't share this belief. I believe you are safer parked out in the middle of nowhere in the dark. That same nut job who can find you in a parking lot is not about to go driving around on dirt roads to see if anyone is parked there. At least that's my belief. You may not share it, and that's fine. Park and camp wherever you feel safe.

I don't go for rest areas either because they have a track record of incidents happening to people in rest areas, especially women travelers.

So, where do I camp? In state or national campgrounds, wildlife sanctuaries, or off on a dirt road somewhere, usually out in the middle of nowhere.

There are definitely times when I stay in a motel. I use Hotels.com because I like their stay 10 nights, get 1 night free deal. So, I book a hotel or motel if:

- The weather is too hot or too cold, or too rainy

- I am in a city and plan to stay awhile

- I'm tired of camping, need a shower, or my body hurts

- I need to do laundry

A word about safety:

When you are a woman traveling alone, it's critical to keep a low profile. Don't tell people you are traveling alone, where you are staying, or any other personal information.

I don't go to bars or get drunk. I'm not preaching but you are on your own, in a city or town you've never been to, and you don't know anyone, so it's not the time to lose control of what you are doing. When you are in control, you are better able to decide which people you want to get to know better.

Travel tip: If you feel vulnerable traveling alone, that's OK. Vulnerability is part of passion, and traveling is a passionate thing to do. You can put one of those family stickers on your vehicle to indicate to others that you are not traveling alone, which can help you feel more secure.

Maintain your connections:

When you are traveling alone, there is a definite sense of disconnection. It feels almost like you are the only one in the world, traveling through space and time. That's why it's critical to keep your connections to loved ones active.

Be on Facebook while you are traveling. You may not have internet a lot of the time, or the internet will be poor. Consider paying to have your phone be a hotspot. It's a little bit of money per month, but it's worth it and has saved me from being without internet. I love the convenience of it, and you will too.

Plan your journey around visiting family members or friends you haven't seen for a long time, or people that are good friends. When you see people you know, it will ground you, so you can continue traveling.

Check in by phone with loved ones. They worry about you, and it's good for both of you to stay connected no matter where you are.

Consider traveling with a pet. I started my trip with my beloved 14-year-old sheltie named Sadie. She didn't make it to the end of the trip. I lost her to bladder cancer about four months in. My Sadie was special, and I will never forget my first traveling buddy.

It took me a solid year to decide on getting another dog. I poured over profiles of rescue dogs, looking for a little buddy I could take care of. Best Friends Animal Society in Kanab, Utah, had my perfect match. I now have Rosie, an 8 year-old sheltie that looks just like Sadie and has many of the same mannerisms. Life is good again.

I highly recommend Best Friends Animal Society if you are looking for a pet. They have 3000 acres and house up to 1600 animals at one time including dogs, cats, horses, pigs, and just about everything else. The dedicated people at Best Friends are wonderful both to you, and your potential pet.

Travel tip: One of the easiest and best ways I stay connected while traveling is to offer to take a photo for someone I don't know. Many couples, families, or singles would love to have more pictures of themselves traveling. It's an easy and quick way to have a connection with a fellow traveler, and it's good manners too.

Practical matters:

You need to have an address to send your mail to. Keep in touch with whomever is nice enough to do this for you.

You will also need to come back occasionally to register your car, vote, go to doctor visits, and take care of any other business. You can't leave it all behind, as tempting as that may be.

Bad things that happened:

Remember when I said you need to take spontaneity with you on your trip? Well, there were many times when I used my spontaneity skillset.

The government shutdown happened smack dab in the middle of my travels. That meant that all of the National Monuments were closed. I did a lot of driving and circling around.

I also did a lot of circling around trying to avoid natural disasters. I traveled through Paradise, California shortly before a massive fire happened there. I tried to travel through the area again but was pushed out by massive flooding. My latest event was camping in Canyonville, Oregon and waking up to flames creeping down the hillside. That was day one of the Canyonville fire.

Besides being driven out by natural disasters, sometimes I was driven out by rude people. Many times it was centered around my furry traveling companion. I believe there are really only two types of people, those who love animals and those who don't. When people see me walking my beautiful, sweet, elderly dog, they either come up and pet her, or they say something harsh.

One incident was a woman, a total stranger, who came up to me smiling down at Sadie and asked how old she was. I replied, "She is 13 and a half years old." The woman replied very curtly "She needs to be put down." Sadie was walking around, alert, and happy, and yet this woman wanted me to end her life because she was old.

Speaking of animals, several times I came very close to driving into an animal on the road. I can't stress enough how many times this will happen to you, and all I can say is, be alert at all times while you are driving. When you travel a lot of miles, you will get tired, so stop and smell the roses, and try not to drive at night.

Good things that happened:

One of the sheer joys of taking a road trip is the unpredictability of it. You never know what you will see. I am originally from Oregon, and bears are not a common sight. So, while driving high up in the Blue Mountains, I looked over and saw a bear! So exciting! He didn't stay for long, kind of shy, but so cute. I love animals, so to see the rich and wonderful amount of wildlife in our country gladdened my heart.

I met many great people on my trip, from all walks of life. They were a walking, talking advertisement for our beautiful country. I smiled at them, and they smiled back. We are all Americans, and we are all part of the human race. When you meet people across the country, you realize just how important it is to get to know your fellow citizens, and learn more about how they view the world and our country.

I have to give a special shout-out to the many dedicated people, often volunteers, who staff our state and national parks and monuments. They work tirelessly to ensure the health of our natural resources, and help travelers enjoy their visit. The same is true of the many people who staff the museums in small towns and large cities. They enjoy history, like I do, and it shows in their smiles.

Along with wonderful people, I have seen an America that is spectacularly beautiful, with open prairies, majestic mountains, and crystal clear rivers. I have seen a small fraction of the history of our country. I have seen the memorials to the brave people who shaped our country. I have fallen in love with America in a way that was not possible sitting in my living room. People ask me, "Would I do it again?" The answer comes easily, "Yes, in a heartbeat."

Bibliography and Further Reading

Bachelor Loop Historic Tour, Willow Creek Reclamation Committee, 2016.

Cliff Palace, Mesa Verde Museum Association

Coquoz, Rene. Tales of Early Leadville. Not Listed, 1997.

Crutchfield, James A. It Happened in Colorado: Remarkable Events That Shaped History. TwoDot, 2017.

Diamond, Jared M. Collapse: How Societies Choose to Fail or Succeed. Penguin Books, 2011.

Donovan, Jim. A Terrible Glory: Custer and the Little Bighorn--the Last Great Battle of the American West. Back Bay Books, 2009.

Enss, Chris. Object, Matrimony: the Risky Business of Mail-Order Matchmaking on the Western Frontier. Globe Pequot Press, 2013.

Enss, Chris. Tales behind the Tombstones. Morris Pub., 2007.

Enss, Chris. The Doctor Wore Petticoats: Women Physicians of the Old West. TwoDot, 2006.

Finch, etc. al.., Jackie. Eyewitness Travel USA. DK Publishing, 2017.

Georgetown Map and Guanella Pass Route, Georgetown Visitor's Center

Golden History Park Walking Guide, Golden History

Houston, Grant E. Historic Homes of Lake City, Colorado. Citizens Printing Company, 2002.

Lake City, Colorado Visitors Guide, Lake City/Hinsdale County Marketing Committee, 2019.

Legendary Leadville, Herald Democrat, 2018.

Leslie, Darlene, et al. The Richest Square Mile on Earth. TB Publishing, 1990.

Mesa Verde , National Park Service

Ouray County Historical Museum Tour Book, Ouray County Historical Society

Rutter, Michael. Bedside Book of Bad Girls: Outlaw Women of the American West. Farcountry Press, 2008.

Smith, B. Ghost Stories of the Rocky Mountains. Lone Pine Pub., 1999.

South Pass City Walking Guide, Friends of South Pass

Varney, Philip. Ghost Towns of the Mountain West: Your Guide to the Hidden History and Old West Haunts of Colorado, Wyoming, Idaho, Montana, Utah, and Nevada. MBI Pub. Co. and Voyageur Press, 2010.

Waters, Stephanie. Colorado Legends & Lore. The History Press, 2014.

Wommack, Linda. Haunted Cripple Creek and Teller County. The History Press, 2018.

Index

About the Author

*J**ulie Bettendorf** is a world traveler with a degree in archaeology and a background in history. She has traveled extensively throughout Egypt, Central America, South America, Europe, and the United Kingdom, visiting archaeological and historical sites all along the way.

Currently, Julie is traveling around the US visiting ghost towns, ancient rock art sites, and archaeological wonders as part of research for her ongoing historical travel series entitled ***Wandering Woman***. Wandering Woman is a set of state-by-state guides, full of photographs, historical anecdotes, and unique tips to help other women travel and explore solo across the US by car. Julie enjoys writing freelance blogs, traveling frequently with her two adult children, and hiking outdoors with her faithful dog companion Rosie.

Also by Julie Bettendorf

W**andering Woman: Colorado* is the fourth book in the ***Wandering Woman Travel Series. The first three books ***Wandering Woman: Montana***, ***Wandering Woman: Utah***, and ***Wandering Woman: Nevada***, are available in ebook and paperback.

Julie has published two children's books in an ongoing, beautifully illustrated travel series entitled *Anthony Ant Goes to France* and *Anthony Ant Goes to Egypt.*

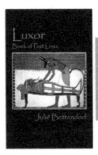

She has also published a work of historical fiction entitled *Luxor: Book of Past Lives* which has recently been released as an audiobook, read by renowned narrator Barry Shannon.

Made in the USA
Las Vegas, NV
29 July 2022

52378572R00096